Introduction

Bill Walton, the National Basketball Association's most valuable player in 1977 and 1978, grew up tall and terrific in Southern California. A high school basketball star in San Diego, he went on in college to lead the UCLA Bruins to three straight national championships and an amazing overall record of eighty-six wins and only four losses. Though hampered by injuries his first two years as a pro, he regained his health in the 1976–77 season and led the Portland Trail Blazers to the championship of the NBA.

A deft shooter, fierce rebounder, great passer, and diehard defender, Bill Walton has earned the reputation of being the best all-around center in basketball history.

Sports Hero

Bill Walton

by Marshall Burchard

G. P. Putnam's Sons · New York

PHOTO CREDITS

Copyright © 1978 by Marshall Burchard
All rights reserved.
Published simultaneously in Canada by
Longman Canada Limited, Toronto,
PRINTED IN THE UNITED STATES OF AMERICA
07210

Library of Congress Cataloging in Publication Data
Burhcard, Marshall.
  Sports hero, Bill Walton.
  (Sports hero biographies)
  SUMMARY: A biography of the captain and central
player of the champion Portland Trail Blazers
basketball team.
  1. Walton, Bill, 1952-   —Juvenile literature.
2. Basketball players—United States—Biography—
Juvenile literature [1. Walton, Bill, 1952-
2. Basketball players] I. Title.
GV884.W3B87   796.32′3′0924 [B] [92]   78-17442
ISBN 0-399-61128-2 lib. bdg.

Contents

Sports Hero

Bill Walton

California Boy

Bill Walton, the best all-around center in basketball and the NBA's most valuable player in 1977 and 1978, comes from Southern California. He was born there November 5, 1952 in the port city of San Diego just a few miles from the Mexican border.

His father, Ted Walton, worked for the San Diego Department of Public

Welfare. His mother, Gloria Walton, was a librarian.

Bill was the second of four children. His brother Bruce was a year older. His sister Cathy was a year younger, and his other brother, Andy, was three years younger.

The Waltons lived in a house on a hill in a suburb of San Diego called La Mesa. Gloria spent a lot of time in the kitchen cooking. Her children had enormous appetites. She fed them a heavy meat diet that often included hot dogs and hamburgers for breakfast as well as steaks and roasts for dinner.

"There is no doubt in my mind," Bill says, "that Glo's cooking is the reason I grew to be six-eleven."

The Waltons did things together. Ted and Gloria took their children on picnics and hikes. In the evenings after dinner Ted played the piano and led the family in song. Later, when the children were old enough to play musical instruments, the Waltons had a five-piece family band. Bill played baritone horn. Bruce played trombone, Cathy drums, Andy saxophone and Ted piano. Ted made all the children take music lessons until they reached the eighth grade.

Ted and Gloria taught their children to play games and encouraged them to compete. They held family foot races and gave prizes to the winners. They had squeezing contests to see who had the strongest grip.

One day Ted offered to give a dollar to any child who could touch the ceiling with his or her hand.

"We had them jumping like maniacs, covering the ceiling with smudges," Gloria recalls. "The contest ended when Bill began touching the ceiling with his elbows."

"I never tried to steer my kids into sports," Ted says. "I encouraged them to play, but only as a broadening experience to complement their music. So wouldn't you know, they all gave up music and wound up in sports!"

Bill's sports career began at the Blessed Sacrament parochial school, which he attended from the fourth through the eighth grade. He played three sports: football, basketball, and baseball. His coach was Frank Graziano, a fireman who volunteered his time to run the school's athletic program.

Bill was shy. He stammered. He was tall and gangly and he stooped when he walked. He didn't look like much of an athlete.

After class at high school.

But when it came time to play he was anything but awkward. In football he was an outstanding end. In basketball he was the team's best ball handler. Because of his height he was used as a center on defense. But to take advantage of his ball-handling skill, coach Graziano had him switch to guard on offense.

Bill was also a good student. He came from a home that was full of books and he enjoyed reading.

He was graduated from Blessed Sacrament in 1966. As he prepared to enter high school, coach Graziano gave him some parting advice. The coach urged Bill to forget about playing the other sports and to concentrate entirely on playing basketball.

Brother Act

Bill went to Helix High School. His big brother, Bruce, was in the class ahead. Although Bruce was a star in football and basketball, Bill took coach Graziano's advice and played only basketball.

As a freshman Bill was almost six feet tall. He made the freshman basketball team with ease and was playing well until he was sidelined by an injury to his left knee.

Doctors operated to remove some torn cartilage. Bill was on crutches for weeks afterwards. Every day for months he did leg exercises to strengthen his knee.

On the campus of Helix High.

The next year, as a six-foot-one-inch sophomore, he spent most of the basketball season on the junior varsity, playing himself back into shape. He joined the varsity for the last six games of the year.

Over the following months he grew half a foot. When he reported for basketball his junior year, he was six feet seven inches tall, a full two inches taller than his brother Bruce, who was playing his final season. The coach, Gordon Nash, made Bill his starting center.

At 185 pounds, Bill was only slightly heavier than he had been the year before. He was a very tall, very skinny boy of seventeen, and he tired easily.

At the start of the season some of the sturdier opposing players tried to shove him around. His burly brother Bruce, who was six-feet-five and weighed 265 pounds, came to the rescue.

"When they would begin to rough up Bill, I would look at coach and he would give me a nod," Bruce remembers.

"When the referee wasn't looking," Gloria Walton recalls, "Bruce would give the player an elbow and let him know that the skinny guy was his kid brother."

"After that," Bruce says, "they wouldn't rough up Bill anymore."

The Walton brothers were the stars of the team. Coach Nash made them

Leaping high for a rebound.

the twin pivots in a high-low post offense. Bill stationed himself near the
basket in a low post position. Bruce
hung out at the top of the key in a
high post.

When the other team played man-
to-man defense, the ball went to Bill

in the low post. With his good moves, his height and jumping ability, and his shooting skill, he easily outplayed the one man guarding him. He scored on hooks, layups, and stuffs.

When the opposing players tried to stop Bill by double- and triple-teaming him, Bruce was free to score on jumpshots from the top of the key or driving layups down the lane.

With Bill and Bruce running the show, Helix High won twenty-nine games and lost only two. In a post-season tournament they won the high school championship of San Diego.

Bill was the team's leading scorer and rebounder. He was named San Diego's best high school center.

Over the summer he took long

bike rides to build up his endurance. When he returned to school for his final year he had grown some more. He was six-feet-ten and weighed over 200 pounds.

Bruce was in his first year of college. But if Bill missed his brother's presence in the lineup it didn't show in his performance. He scored a total of 985 points, the most points ever scored in a season by a San Diego high school player. He had an average of twenty-nine points and twenty-four rebounds a game. He sank more than seventy percent of his shots from the floor.

Helix High won all thirty-three of its games. In the final of the postseason tournament, the team defeated

Chula Vista High and won the regional championship of San Diego for the second year in a row.

Bill dominated the championship game. He had twenty-six points, thirty-three rebounds, and sixteen blocked shots.

College recruiters from all over the

Helix High School's Athlete of the Year.

country were hot on his trail. Among the men who scouted him was Denny Crum, then an assistant to coach John Wooden of the University of California at Los Angeles.

"Coach," Crum told Wooden after watching Bill play, "I've just seen the greatest high school prospect ever."

That was quite a statement, especially coming from Crum, since he had previously scouted Kareem Abdul-Jabbar when he was a high school player in New York. Coach Wooden reminded him about Kareem.

"Yeah," Crum said, "but this kid is better."

Wooden stepped into his office.

"Come inside," he said, "and close the door."

3

The Walton Gang

Bill was graduated from high school in 1970. He spent the summer in Europe playing exhibition games for a touring United States team sponsored by the Amateur Athletic Union. In the fall he registered for his freshman year at the University of California at Los Angeles.

He picked UCLA for several reasons. One was its location. He liked living in Southern California and wanted to remain in the area.

The school also offered some courses that interested him, and it had the best college basketball program in the country.

The UCLA Bruins had been national champions every year but one since Bill was in sixth grade. They had won the title six times in seven years, including the last four years in a row. One of Bill's heroes when he was in high school, Kareem Abdul-Jabbar, had led the Bruins to three of those titles.

Bill's brother Bruce was at UCLA, too. But the brother act that had worked so well on the court in high school was over. Just as Bill had given up football to concentrate on basketball, so Bruce gave up basketball to concentrate on football. He was a tackle at UCLA, and when he finished college he played pro football for the Dallas Cowboys.

Bill was a sensational center on a sensational freshman team that included high-scoring forward Keith "Silk" Wilkes and sharp-shooting point guard Greg Lee.

The Baby Bruins got off to a slow start in their opening game when they beat El Camino Junior College by a mere twenty-two points, 78–56. In their second game, against Valley State College, they picked up the tempo of their attack and won 106–

60. They continued to score over one hundred points in game after game as they piled up one lopsided victory after another. They beat one team, Chaffey College, by seventy-seven points, 128–51.

The UCLA freshmen won all twenty games. Bill scored a total of 362 points and grabbed 320 rebounds, an average of eighteen points and sixteen rebounds per game. He sank sixty-two percent of his shots from the floor. After the season he was awarded a trophy for being the most valuable player on the team.

In his sophomore year at UCLA Bill won national fame for his play as starting center on the varsity. At six-eleven he was one of the country's tallest players. He had all the skills and he played with fierce intensity. He covered the court, leaping up to block shots and grab rebounds, diving to the floor after loose balls, feeding teammates with pinpoint passes, and scoring on hook shots, jump shots and stuffs. He intimidated his rivals and dominated every game.

His favorite play was the fast break. He liked it because it involved the whole team. His role was to grab the rebound and start the fast break by firing a pass to a speedy guard at midcourt. The guard could drive to the basket, pull up for a jumper, or pass off to a teammate for an open shot.

Taking down a rebound against Loyola. The Bruins won
the game 87–73 in Chicago.

"On defense I make a point of knowing where all my guys are, all the time," Bill said, "so when I get the ball, even while facing the basket, I am thinking about the fast break. When I'm trailing the play and see everything materialize in front of me—Wow! That pleases me the most."

"We are only now beginning to realize how good he is," said Bruin guard Greg Lee. "With Bill back there on defense, the rest of us can afford to gamble, and we can cheat getting out on the fast break."

"He's as fine a team player as you'll ever see," said UCLA head coach John Wooden. "He knows there's more to the game than scoring."

UCLA opened the 1971–72 season by demolishing Citadel, 105–49. The Bruins were off and running. With their lanky, redheaded center controlling the boards and launching the fast break, they won a string of easy victories.

Sportswriters heaped attention on Bill. They dubbed the team the Walton Gang, and compared Bill to the most famous big men in the history of the game: Bill Russell, Wilt Chamberlain, and Kareem Abdul-Jabbar. Bill was disturbed by all the acclaim.

"It hurts me when people talk as if I'm the only player on the team,"

Moving in on the basket in the tournament final.

he said. "I don't like to be singled out as an individual because we don't play as individuals, we play as a team."

The Bruins marched through the season without a defeat. Bill averaged twenty-one points and fifteen rebounds a game. He hit on sixty-five percent of his field goal attempts.

In the postseason National Collegiate Athletic Association tournament, UCLA beat Louisville in the semi-final round, 96–77. Bill had thirty-three points and twenty-one rebounds.

After the game he received praise from the new Louisville coach, the man who had scouted him in high school, Denny Crum.

Sidelined by an injury, Bill coaches his teammates from the bench.

"One thing that goes unnoticed," Crum said, "is that Bill's smart. He's always in the right place, and he's always talking to his teammates so they'll be in the right place. He's a great leader."

The Bruins beat a stubborn Florida State team in the final, 81–76. Bill was high scorer with twenty-four points and was named most valuable player in the tournament.

It was UCLA's thirtieth victory of the year and it brought them their sixth straight national championship. For Bill it was the third year in a row in which his team was undefeated. Over the three years, which began when he was a high school senior, his teams had a combined record of 83–0.

Eighty-eight Straight

Bill lived quietly in a rented room near the UCLA campus. He was a serious student, specializing in history, with a B-plus average.

When he wasn't playing basketball he was usually studying. Sometimes to let off pressure, he rode his bicycle to the beach and gazed out at the Pacific.

Shooting for two of his record forty-four points against
Memphis State.

Bill began meditating, stopped eating meat, and became a vegetarian. He tried acupuncture as well as ice packs for his sore knees.

In his junior year UCLA again won all thirty of its games. Bill capped another great season with an amazing performance in the final game of the NCAA tournament. He scored forty-four points, hitting on twenty-one of twenty-two field goal attempts. The Bruins beat Memphis State 87–66, capturing their seventy-fifth straight victory and their seventh national title in a row.

"That was the best performance I've ever seen," said the Memphis State coach, Gene Bartow. "I've

Accepting the Amateur Athletic Union 1973 Sullivan Award as the nation's top amateur athlete. Bill edged 1972 Olympic 800-meter track champion Dave Wottle by 46 points in the AAU voting.

never seen a player so dominating as Walton.''

At the end of his junior year the Philadelphia 76ers offered Bill $3 million to quit college and turn pro. He

Walton soars to snatch a rebound.

declined the offer because he wanted to finish school.

That summer a freak accident almost cost him his life. Bill was stung by a bee while riding on his bicycle. He had such a strong reaction to the sting that only a shot of antitoxin kept him from dying.

He was fully recovered by the time he started his senior year. That winter the Bruins extended their unbeaten streak into its third season.

Bill's parents drove up to Los Angeles to watch many of the games. They were proud of their son, but Gloria Walton worried that his team might be too successful for its own good.

"Well, I just think winning all the time is immoral," she said.

UCLA had won eighty-eight straight games, an all-time college record, when Notre Dame finally snapped the streak in January with a

Laughter on the Bruin bench during UCLA's 111–59 romp over St. Bonaventure.

Tipping in two points as the Bruins easily beat Notre Dame 94–75 in Los Angeles. Going up with Walton is Bill Paterno.

71–70 win. For Bill it was the end of a 157-game winning streak that had started in his junior year of high school.

The Bruins dropped two more close games, losing to Oregon, 51–46, and to Oregon State, 61–57. Their bid for an eighth straight national title failed when they were edged out in the final game of the NCAA tournament by North Carolina State, 80–77, in double overtime.

In his three seasons on the varsity Bill scored 1,767 points, a total second only to Kareem Abdul-Jabbar's 2,325. Bill's 1,370 rebounds were the most in UCLA history. He averaged twenty points a game, set an NCAA

record by making sixty-five percent
of his field goal attempts, and led the
Bruins to a three-year won-lost record of 86–4.

Walton directs his teammates on the floor.

"There have been many great players in the game, but not many great team players," said coach Wooden. "Walton is a very great team player."

Captain Flake

On finishing college in 1974, Bill signed a contract for $2.5 million to play five years for the Portland Trail Blazers. At the time, the Blazers were the National Basketball Association's newest and weakest team. By adding Walton to their lineup they hoped to become an instant contender for the playoffs.

Bill spent the summer of 1974 settling into a house in Portland, riding his bicycle, and backpacking in the Oregon wilderness.

During the summer he ate only raw fruits and vegetables. Sometimes he fasted. When he reported to the Blazers for practice in September he weighed 216 pounds, fourteen pounds less than he weighed at UCLA.

The Blazer coach, Lenny Wilkens, was worried by the weight loss. But in his first pro game, a preseason exhibition with the Los Angeles Lakers, Bill looked good, scoring twenty-six points.

A week later, in another exhibition game, he had his first encounter with

Guarded by John Gianelli, Walton calls for the ball in an
exhibition game against the New York Knicks.

Maneuvering for position under the basket, Bill tries to block out Kareem.

his high school hero, the seven-foot-two-inch Kareem Abdul-Jabbar, who was then playing for the Milwaukee Bucks.

Jabbar looked bored as he went to work against the Portland rookie.

Kareem scored on a jump shot, a stuff, another jump shot, a layup, and a hook. As the first quarter ended he tossed in a fifteen-foot skyhook, turned on his heel and walked to the bench. Bill just stood there looking at the basket, shaking his head in disbelief.

They were on the court together a total of twenty-seven minutes. During that time Kareem outscored Bill 28–8. Afterwards Bill's face was red.

"Kareem is the best I've ever seen," he said.

"It's the first time he's ever played me," said Kareem, "and the first time is always tough. It's always tougher for the younger man because the

Walton concentrates on the basketball during a game against Detroit.

older man knows what he's doing. I could tell him but you have to learn through experience. He's got to learn to face the basket. But he's quick and he rebounds well and he tries to help his teammates.''

Blazer forward Sidney Wicks, also a former UCLA star, tried to warn Bill of what to expect as a rookie in the NBA.

"I told him it's not fun and games anymore, that you *work* basketball, that you can't win all the time because it's not good old UCLA, that you've got to grow up. But it's one of those things you have to experience yourself.''

Early in the season Bill missed two games because he had the flu. The night he returned to the lineup he jammed a finger and was out of action for another week. Then a bone spur in his ankle sidelined him for twenty games.

The rainy Oregon winter depressed him. So did the lack of harmony on the Portland club.

"Bill loves the game," said his college coach, John Wooden, "but only as a team game. He is very impatient and gets more upset than most people when he feels the game isn't being played right."

One night Blazer guard Geoff Petrie launched a shot that was too long for Bill's liking. When the ball bounced off the rim, Bill grabbed the rebound. But instead of stuffing

Bill cuts up with Blazer guard Greg Lee, former UCLA
teammate and roomie.

Popping a short jumper against the Knicks at Madison
Square Garden. The player on the right is Earl the Pearl
Monroe.

it home he called time out and scolded Petrie for making a selfish play.

Because of illness and injury, Bill missed playing in more than half of Portland's games. In the games he did play he averaged just under thirteen points and thirteen rebounds.

His teammates, expecting him to be their leader, were disappointed when he rode the bench while their losses continued to mount. They thought he wasn't hurt so badly that he couldn't play.

"He was going to be the *man*," said forward John Johnson. "This is all a big letdown."

One morning at practice, after the coach had left, Bill suddenly found

Taking aim on a free throw.

himself surrounded by a bunch of grinning Blazers.

"Let's take our frustrations out on Captain Flake," one of them said, firing a basketball at Bill's head. For the next few moments Bill ducked and cursed as his teammates laughed and peppered him with basketballs.

Bill was so unhappy at Portland that he asked to be traded to the Los Angeles Lakers. The Blazers refused to part with him.

He had come to them as one of the greatest college players of all time. But as he reached the end of his rookie year people wondered if he would have the stamina and the will-power to survive another season in the pros.

Battling Back

At the end of his rookie year Bill was down to 205 pounds.

"His legs are so skinny they're turning blue," said teammate Sidney Wicks.

Coach Wilkens told Bill to gain some weight over the summer.

"I want the extra weight on him not so he can shove people around, but because you have to have strength and stamina to play eighty-two games," the coach said. "You have to have some weight. Big guys like him can lose eight to ten pounds in a game."

Maintaining his vegetarian diet, Bill stuffed himself at every meal. He ate huge amounts of potatoes—as much as seven pounds for breakfast. He also ate lots of pasta, as well as nuts, seeds, grains, fruits, and vegetables.

He lifted weights, rode his bicycle, hiked, played volleyball, and shot baskets. When he reported to the Blazer training camp the following fall, he weighed in at 250 pounds.

Blocking a shot by the Warriers' Phil Smith.

"I'm going to be much more aggressive this year," he said. "I want to show what Bill Walton can do."

"I like what I see," said coach Wilkens. "He'll probably play at 240 once he's through with two-a-day workouts."

But Bill had to miss the early practices because of a broken toe. Once the season started he continued to be plagued by injuries. He missed thirty-one games. When he did play he was never 100 percent.

Team spirit sank to a new low. The players bickered with one another and with their coach. Bill was singled out for much of the criticism.

"I think he was overwhelmed by

Driving on Otto Moore of the New Orleans Jazz.

the atmosphere," says his Blazer teammate Larry Steele.

Portland had the worst won-lost record in the West. At the end of the 1975–76 season coach Wilkens was fired. He was replaced by the coach of the Buffalo Braves, Jack Ramsay.

"I'm a Bill Walton man," Ramsay declared when he arrived in Portland to begin his new job.

Ramsay's first move was to sell or trade all the players who had been causing friction. To take their place he assembled a group of cooperative players whose skills were well suited to Bill's favorite style of offense, the fast break.

From the American Basketball

In a huddle with coach Jack Ramsey.

Association came the speedy, sure-handed guard, Dave Twardzik, and the big, power forward, Maurice Lucas. Completing the starting five,

At training camp Walton (left) and Maurice Lucas stretch their muscles.

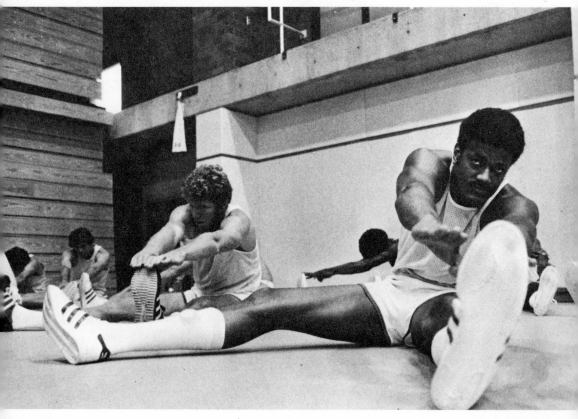

in addition to Bill, were guard Lionel Hollins and forward Bob Gross.

Coach Ramsay's plan was simple. When the other team took a shot, Walton and Lucas would climb the boards for the rebound. At the same moment Gross, Twardzik, and Hollins would quit playing defense and dash up the court to receive the outlet pass that would begin the fast break.

The plan worked beautifully. With Bill Walton free of injuries for the first time in his pro career, the Blazers began tearing up the league with their scorching fast break.

They scored 145 points in a game with the Indiana Pacers, and 146 points in a game with the Philadelphia 76ers. Against the Atlanta

Hawks they pumped in forty-five points in the first quarter.

"Look up there," Atlanta coach Hubie Brown told his players, pointing at the scoreboard. "Do you know what that means? That means 180 points at the end."

The Blazers won thirteen straight games at home and took an early lead in the Pacific Division race with a record of fifteen wins, six losses.

Everybody on the Portland team contributed to the victories. But the man who contributed the most was Big Bill. When the situation demanded it, he could take command of a game, as he did in the fourth quarter against the Phoenix Suns when he scored eleven points in

Backed up by teammates Lloyd Neal and Bob Grosse,
Bill argues with an official over a call.

seven minutes to nail down a 113–99 win.

"The guy just keeps storming at you," said the Suns' center, Alvan Adams.

A quarter of the way through the season Bill was leading the NBA in rebounds and blocked shots, while scoring an average of twenty-one points a game.

"I'm just healthy, that's all," he said, explaining the striking improvement in his performance. "For two years I wasn't able to run up and down the court freely without making a conscious effort out of it. Without *thinking* about it. That's no way to play basketball.

"I love this game. I always have.

Walton scores on a left-handed hook over Buffalo's Jim McDaniels.

And I always knew how good I was. It's just that when you're going up against guys you know you can take anytime, but you can't because of a bad ankle or too much weight or a broken hand or something else, it is too discouraging. And not any fun.''

NBA Champs

Bill was the Portland team captain and he took the title seriously. Out on the court he constantly gave his teammates instructions and advice.

"In practice I'll say things to them all the time," he said. "I'll tell them things I think will help them in a way they can accept. And they do it to me too. They help me. They're watching

Blocking San Antonio's Coby Dietrick from inbounding the ball.

me so they see my mistakes. Like if
I'm shooting poorly and they notice
I'm not concentrating on the rim. I
like to hear a critique from anyone
who knows what he's talking about.''

Portland finished the 1976–77 season in second place in the Pacific Division behind the Los Angeles Lakers. In the early playoff rounds the Blazers defeated the Chicago Bulls and the Denver Nuggets. In the semifinal series they met the Los Angeles Lakers.

It was a classic duel between the two big men: the Blazers' Walton, twenty-four years old and playing his third season as a pro, and the Lakers' Abdul-Jabbar, thirty and playing his eighth. In previous encounters Kareem had usually outplayed Bill. This time things were different.

Blazermania swept Portland. When the Blazers edged the Lakers on their

homecourt in Los Angeles, the radio dispatcher at police headquarters in Portland broadcast the good news:

"Information to all cars. The Trail Blazers just won, 99–97."

The Blazers took the first two games out of seven and were leading in the final moments of the third when the Lakers fought back to within two points. Then Walton and Abdul-Jabbar put on a show. As the teams raced up and down the court, there was a flurry of scoring in which the two big men made all the baskets.

During this torrid stretch Bill outscored Kareem five baskets to three. The Blazers won the game and went on to sweep the Lakers in four straight.

The Blazers then played the favored Philadelphia 76ers in the finals. The Sixers won the first two games on their homecourt in Philadelphia. The Blazers won the next two games on their homecourt in Portland.

The fifth game was in Philadelphia. Although Julius Erving scored thirty-seven points for the Sixers, the Blazers broke the homecourt advantage with a 110–104 victory and took a three–two lead in the series. Bill had twenty-four rebounds.

The sixth game was in Portland. When the final quarter began, the

Taking a rebound away from the Sixers' Julius Erving.

Blazers were ahead by nine points. But led by Julius Erving, who had forty points for the night, the Sixers closed the gap.

With seconds remaining and the score Portland 109, Philadelphia 107, George McGinnis of the Sixers missed a shot that would have tied the game. Walton, collecting his twenty-third rebound, tipped the ball to a Blazer guard, Johnny Davis, who dribbled until time ran out.

After losing the first two games, the Blazers had beaten the Sixers four in a row. They were champions of the NBA.

Bill stripped off his jersey, wadded it into a ball and threw it into the

stands. Then he headed for the locker
room, hugging and kissing his teammates as he went.

"Winning the NCAA was nice,"

he said, "but this was nicer. Here we have the best players in the game involved and that makes it better."

Bill took a drink of fruit juice.

"Man," he said, "I feel good all over."

About the Author

Marshall Burchard, a writer and sports fan, lives in New York.

He has recently written Sports Hero biographies on Muhammad Ali, Reggie Jackson, Dr. J., Jimmy Connors, Fred Lynn, Pete Rose, Rick Barry, Fran Tarkenton, Mario Andretti, Joe Morgan, and Rod Carew.

He has been the coauthor of numerous other Sports Hero biographies, among them *Joe Namath, Brooks Robinson, Bobby Orr, Roger Staubach, Larry Csonka, Billie Jean King, O.J. Simpson, Phil Esposito,* and *Richard Petty.*

13745

92
Walton

Burchard, Marshall
Sports hero: Bill Walton

DATE DUE		
JAN 0 2	APR 4 '88	
MAR 2 5 1986	FEB 28 '89	
MAR 2 6	MAR 14 '90	
NOV. 03	NOV 30 '90	
	DEC 19 '90	
JAN. 26	NOV 22 '93	
MAR 12 '87	DEC 16 '95	
APR 6 '87	FEB 2 2 1996	
	DEC 0 2 1998	
MAY 15 '87	JAN 0 7 2005	
OCT 6 '87	JAN 2 1 2005	
JAN 22 '00	FEB 0 4 2005	
MAR 17 '88		

MEDIALOG 2001 Gilbert Ave.
Cincinnati, Ohio 45202